margaritas

RYLAND
PETERS
& SMALL
LONDON NEW YORK

margaritas

and other tequila cocktails

ben reed

photography by william lingwood

For Amy

Senior Designer Catherine Griffin
Editor Miriam Hyslop
Production Patricia Harrington
Art Director Gabriella Le Grazie
Publishing Director Alison Starling

Mixologist Ben Reed
Stylist Helen Trent

First published in the United States in 2004 by
Ryland Peters & Small, Inc.
519 Broadway
5th Floor
New York NY 10012
www.rylandpeters.com

10 9 8 7 6 5 4 3 2 1

Printed in China.

Library of Congress Cataloging-in-Publication Data
Reed, Ben.
  Margaritas and other tequila cocktails / Ben
Reed.– 1st ed.
    p. cm.
Includes index.
  ISBN 1-84172-586-2
  1. Margaritas. 2. Tequila. 3. Cocktails. I. Title.
TX951.R35522 2003
641.8'74–dc22
                                          2003015925

contents

tequila history

Tequila and tequila-based cocktails have always had, how shall I put this, a bit of a reputation. Tequila is the drink of Mexico and perhaps it is the country's turbulent history that lends this drink its roguish image. This was certainly the case during the Mexican revolution, when men wearing bandaleros, sombreros, and large moustaches sipped tequila in times of exaltation or catastrophe. Retaining its tempestuous past, tequila has moved on and can be seen today decorating the back bars of cantinas, style bars, pubs, clubs, and hotel bars alike.

People everywhere are drinking tequila—from the best-known tequila brands to the rarer tequilas revered by connoisseurs. Tequila has planted itself firmly in the consciousness of the global alcoholic beverages market, and is respected and adored in America, as well as in fifty other countries.

Tequila's origins in Mexico were humble. Approximately 70 per cent of Mexico's territory has an arid or semi-desert climate in which a vast variety of plants grow. The majority of these plants were known as "magueys," later known as "agave." The maguey was used for a number of different purposes by the pre-hispanic American people. Clothes and household utensils were created using the fibers of the plant but more importantly (for our purposes anyway), they used the sap as a beverage.

I may as well, at this early stage, clear up a few fallacies surrounding tequila. The agave plant is not a cactus, despite its appearance, but a member of the lily genus. Within its mass of sharp spiny stems lies the heart (or *piña*, Spanish for "pineapple"). When pierced, the pineapple-shaped center releases a sap that you can drink. Leave the liquid for a few hours, however, and it starts to ferment and turn into alcohol.

This alcoholic version of agave juice was called *pulque* and for the next three hundred years was the traditional drink of Mexico. Tequila was to arrive later on the scene.

Years before the invention of distillation, indigenous farmers discovered their own method of producing alcohol. The *jimadors* (agave harvesters) would discard the remains of the large plants into deep pits. The story goes that one day a fire stared in one of these pits. The impact of the heat on the juice transformed it into an alcoholic drink named *mezcal*.

All tequila is mezcal but not all mezcal is tequila. Tequila production is subject to regulations, similar to those of champagne and cognac. According to the Mexican government, tequila must be made from the juice of agave plants grown in one of five Mexican states, contain at least 51 per cent pure agave juice, and be distilled twice.

With the advent of distillation, the method of production has been modernized. Today, the hearts of the agave plant are heated by steam at a very high temperature for up to a day and a half. The hearts are then crushed to release the juice, which is subsequently fermented.

The fermented liquid is filtered to rid the mixture of the fibrous residue and any other impurities. Once done, the must (resultant liquid) is ready for distillation.

Modern-day distillation takes place in huge stills into which steam is pumped. Often the wash is processed twice to ensure distillation is thorough. The steam forces the alcohol up through the vat into a type of spout, where it is chilled and collected.

the agave plant is not a cactus, despite its appearance, but a member of the lily genus

When the tequila leaves the still, it is clear looking. This type of tequila is called *blanco* (white) or *plata* (silver). It is from this form that various types of tequila are made.

"Gold" tequila is called *joven abocado* in Mexico (roughly translated as "young and medium sweet"). The only difference between "gold" and "white" tequila is the addition of coloring and a small amount of sweetening agent—often caramel—which both colors and sweetens the drink.

The best-quality tequilas are aged in wooden containers. The official terms for these tequilas are *reposado* (rested) and *añejo* (aged). Tequilas described as "rested" must, somewhat confusingly, also be aged, but for a shorter period of time. These tequilas sit in large wooden tanks, some holding as much as about 8,000 U.S. gallons, for a minimum of two months. After two months the tequila can be called

all you need to create a decent
margarita is good-quality tequila,
limes, and orange-flavored liqueur

reposado but more often they are left for four to eight months (anything up to one year is acceptable). *Añejo* tequila is any tequila that has been aged for more than one year in wooden tanks or barrels.

The type of barrel used for aging has a huge effect on the resultant tequila. The barrel's age and its previous use (some tequila producers use barrels previously used by whiskey makers from Tennessee) are both important since they impart different flavors to the drink. Others experiment with oak barrels or barrels charred on the inside to create their distinctive taste (new barrels have the most flavor).

After aging, the tequila is prepared for bottling. With both "aged" and "rested" tequilas, blending is commonplace. As is the case with blended whiskey, the age of the youngest blend used in the mix will be the age of the total blend printed on the bottle.

The person responsible for blending is the most important in the distillery—known as the master blender, his or her job is to maintain the consistency of the various tequilas. Aroma, taste, and appearance are the three main variables, and although taste and appearance can be altered by using coloring or flavoring additives, to get the aroma exactly right the blender has to rely on one thing: his or her nose.

Next, the tequila is bottled and labeled. Tequila bottles can be as colorful and exciting as the drink itself but be warned: expensive tequila is sometimes priced according to the intricacy of its bottle's design.

A common myth is that tequila bottles house a worm. The "worm" seen in the bottom of the bottle of mezcal is actually a butterfly that, in its larval stage, can live in certain types of agave. The larva has long been known to be a nutritional source of food. One day a manufacturer decided to put one in a bottle with the idea that the living larva would ward off any evil spirits. This fascinated the outside world, which began to consume the larva on finishing the bottle for this reason, but no doubt also due to the worm's reputed aphrodisiac quality!

And so, to the good stuff—you've sat patiently through the theory class but you'll have noticed that this is a book about the margarita and some of the other cocktails related to tequila. Originally, the book started as a margaritas-only zone but during the research for the book (aahh the research) I came across a number of tequila-based gems, and during a little experimentation period (mmmm experimentation) I realized that tequila was a willing and surprisingly versatile ingredient when it came to substituting it for other liquors in different classic

cocktails (I dare you to dislike the Herba Buena on page 44, the tequila version of the Mojito).

So what started as an exploration into the margarita became something a little broader—although you will notice that there will always be similarities in the formulas used in tequila cocktails (look at the balance of sweet versus sour).

The margarita hasn't changed much over the years. Invented by any number of people, it has survived numerous nips and tucks to retain its fierce identity. All you need to create a decent margarita is good-quality tequila, limes, and orange-flavored liqueur (preferably a reputable brand like Cointreau or Grand Marnier).

The trick with making margaritas for others is asking the correct questions: "On the rocks or straight up?", "With a salt rim or without?", and most importantly "How do you like yours?"

In a perfect world, everyone should have the opportunity to order and receive a personalized margarita. Sadly this isn't practical in a busy bar, but there's no excuse not to experiment at home. Let me explain: Within the boundaries of the three ingredients used in the margarita there are a number of ways to make the resultant drink taste different.

The first and most obvious way to alter the taste of your drink is to try different brands and ages of tequila. Secondly, you can experiment with your choice of sour: Do you use freshly squeezed lime juice? Where are the limes from? Do you use sour mix? (Not if you can help it— I certainly wouldn't recommend it.) Thirdly, vary the type of sweetener. Triple sec is the most obvious choice but if you want to upgrade your margarita, try using Cointreau or Grand Marnier to create a richer concoction. Finally, think about the ratio of tequila to sour and sweet. Any combination of these variables will result in a very different taste.

For the young (and strong) at heart try the Flavored Margaritas (pages 30–43). A worthy replacement for rum in the summer cocktail stakes. Blend these drinks for the ultimate summer chill or shake them over ice. Or experiment with the Substitutions (pages 44–53): well-known cocktails with tequila substituted for their regular alcohol.

With luck, the forthcoming pages will stimulate your taste buds and your curiosity alike. Tequila has proved to be a worthy travel companion over the last six months of writing. Here's hoping it proves itself worthy of your time.

on the rocks or straight up? with a salt rim or without?

cocktail basics

Equipment

The first thing any aspiring bartender should acquire is a *measure* (jigger). The modern dual-measure jigger measures both 2 oz. and 1 oz. (a double and a single measure). It is essential when mixing these recipes for the first time to follow the guidelines. The *shaker* is the second most important piece of equipment for a bartender. Also very important when dealing with the margarita is a *blender*. Little tip: When using a blender, only use crushed ice (wrap ice in a clean dishtowel or bag and hit it with a rolling pin!); this will preserve the blender's blades. The *barspoon*, with its long spiraling handle, is useful for stirring drinks and for the gentle pouring required for layered drinks. The "wrong," flat end can be used for muddling or crushing herbs, etc. A *muddler* is a wooden pestle for mixing or crushing sugar cubes, limes, and herbs, etc. A *mixing glass* with strainer is used for making drinks that are stirred, not shaken.

Glasses

The margarita can be served in a number of different glasses; either in a *rocks glass* if served on the rocks or in a *margarita coupette* (or in some instances a *martini glass*) if served straight up. Frozen margaritas tend to need slightly larger glasses, a *hurricane glass* should be large enough. The *highball* should be at least 10 oz. The *shot glass* comes in a number of shapes and sizes, any is acceptable. When selecting a rocks glass, I tend to prefer those with a thick bottom and heavy solid feel. The margarita glass can be as ornate or as plain as you see fit (see page 17). You can frost your serving glasses by leaving them in the freezer for an hour before use.

Techniques

There are six basic ways of creating a cocktail: shaking, blending, stirring over ice, layering, building, and muddling. Whichever method you are using, accurately measure the ingredients first to get that all-important balance of tastes right. If you would rather try guesswork, just see how much practice it takes to get the quantity right to fill the glass exactly.

Shaking is a more aggressive way to combine ingredients and should be treated as such—so put your back into it. Add the ingredients to the shaker and fill it with ice. The shaking movement should be sharp and fairly assertive, but do remember to keep your hands on both parts of the shaker or at least a finger on the cap. Five or six aggressive shakes should be enough to frost the shaker (a sign that the drink is ready). Drinks containing cream and juices should be either shaken for slightly longer than the usual ten seconds or blended.

Blending involves pouring all the ingredients into a blender, adding crushed ice, and flicking the switch on. **Stirring** is the best method when you want to retain the clarity and strength of the alcohol. Use an ice-filled mixing glass and stir carefully to avoid chipping the ice and diluting the drink. **Layering** is the technique used for drinks such as La Cucaracha (page 60). With the flat end of a barspoon resting on the surface of the alcohol at the bottom of the glass, pour each of the remaining liquors, in turn, down the handle of the spoon. This keeps the ingredients separate and allows them to be tasted one at a time.

The process of **building** a cocktail just requires adding the measured ingredients to the appropriate glass, with ice, and giving it a quick stir before serving. The **muddling** technique involves using the flat end of a barspoon or a muddler to mix or crush ingredients such as fruit or herbs, and allow the flavors to be released gently.

Extras

For a **salt-rimmed glass**, simply wipe a lime around the rim of the glass. Turn the glass upsidedown and rub the rim of it in a bowl of salt. Continuing to hold the glass upsidedown, wipe the inside with a napkin to ensure the salt only coats the outside of the rim, and doesn't drop in to the drink. For a **lime** or **orange zest**, take a sharp knife and gently skim a length of peel from the fruit—the zest should be fine, with no pith. Squeeze the zest over the drink, wipe it around the rim, and then drop it into the liquid. To make **simple syrup** stir 1lb. of sugar into 1 cup of water, bring to the boil, stirring vigorously. Leave to cool. One last consideration is the **ice** you will be using to chill your cocktails. Where possible, use large, dry ice cubes.

Opposite clockwise from top left: **classic margarita coupette, margarita coupette, highball glass, rocks glass, shot glasses**

the originals

The margarita is a classic cocktail that has been around since the first half of the last century—that much is known. However, as is generally the case with cocktails, there is some confusion as to who exactly invented the drink. Each version of events sounds plausible enough but I am sure that no one was taking notes! Take your pick from the possibilities opposite—my advice would be to choose the story you find the most romantic.

sames Hacienda in Acapulco, Mexico, c.1948.

Margarita Sames, an American socialite, wanted to impress her celebrity friends (including John Wayne) at a party. She mixed tequila with lime and added some of her favorite liqueur, Cointreau.

negrete Garci Crespo Hotel in Pueblo, Mexico, 1936.

Danny Negrete created the margarita with a salt rim for his girlfriend. The young lady had a passion for dipping her fingers into salt but knew it didn't look good! This was quite a novel idea at the time.

morales Tommy's Place, El Paso, Texas, U.S.A., 1942.

Bartender Pancho Morales, created the margarita when asked to mix a Magnolia. Unsure of the exact recipe, Morales made one up, adding tequila and lime to Cointreau. Keeping with the flower theme, he named the drink margarita—the Spanish word for daisy.

derlesse & underwood Tail o' the Cock, Los Angeles, U.S.A., c.1950.

The margarita was made popular at the Tail o' the Cock by a young bartender, Derlesse. When Vernon Underwood, president of Cuervo Tequila distribution, discovered that the margarita was responsible for a huge increase in Cuervo sales, he began to market the drink.

herrera Rancho La Gloria Bar, Rosarito Beach, Tijuana, Mexico, 1938.

Bar owner Danny Herrera created the drink for a showgirl, Marjorie King, who was allergic to all hard liquors except tequila. He named his creation margarita, the Spanish version of Marjorie.

classic margaritas

All you need to create a margarita is good-quality tequila, lime, and orange-flavored liqueur. Yet within the boundaries of these ingredients you can make your drink taste quite different. The type of tequila, the choice of sour, the brand of sweetener and the ratio of all three influence the final flavor. There is no such thing as the perfect margarita and the only person who can judge the levels of perfection is its recipient. Here are some simple recipes to get you started on the road of experimentation.

standard

2 oz. gold tequila

scant oz. triple sec

1 oz. fresh lime juice

lime wheel, to garnish

salt (for the glass)

simple

2 oz. tequila

scant oz. orange juice

1 oz. fresh lime juice

lime wheel, to garnish

salt (for the glass)

sames

1 oz. gold tequila

1 oz. Cointreau

1 oz. fresh lime juice

lime wheel, to garnish

salt (for the glass)

strong

2 oz. tequila

1 oz. Grand Marnier

1 oz. fresh lime juice

lime wheel, to garnish

salt (for the glass)

Add all the ingredients to a shaker filled with ice. Shake sharply and strain into a salt-rimmed, frosted margarita glass. Garnish with a lime wheel.
OR
For frozen margaritas, add all the ingredients to a blender, add one scoop of crushed ice and blend for 20 seconds. Pour into a margarita coupette, and garnish with a lime wheel.

Depending on the method of production and age, tequila yields an abundance of different flavors. This chapter includes some of my favorite fine tequila brands mixed with a delicate balance of sour and sweetness. From the sensational 200th anniversary José Cuervo Reserva de la Familia tequila, used in the 24 Carat Gold Reserva (page 28), to the quality Patrón Añejo found in La Margarita de le Patrón (below), you will discover just how the brand of tequila can influence the taste of your margarita. Each of the tequila brands used in this chapter should be readily available in most specialty liquor shops.

the premium margaritas

la margarita de le patrón

Patrón rightfully stands up as a tequila to be counted. But be warned, its decanter-type bottle may have upped the price on this expensive tequila. Mixed with Citronage (a premium orange liqueur), this margarita is the drink you'd choose if money were no object.

2 oz. Patrón Añejo tequila
1½ oz. Citronage
scant oz. fresh lime juice
salt (for the glass)

Add all the ingredients to a shaker filled with ice. Shake sharply and strain into a salt-rimmed, frosted margarita coupette.

horny toad

Made using Sauza Hornitos, the Horny Toad is named after the creature used to exemplify ugliness in Mexico. Are they saying drinking tequila makes you unattractive? (I've always found everyone much more attractive when I've been drinking tequila!)

1½ oz. **Sauza Hornitos tequila**

1 oz. **Cointreau**

2 oz. **fresh lime or lemon juice**

lime wedge, to garnish

salt (for the glass)

Add all the ingredients to a shaker filled with ice. Shake sharply and strain into a salt-rimmed, rocks glass filled with ice. Garnish with a lime wedge.

conmemorativo triple triple

Triple-distilled Cointreau and triple-distilled Sauza Conmemorativo, mixed with freshly squeezed lemon juice, provides the balance this cocktail needs. Sauza Conmemorativo was introduced to the market as the demand for premium tequila rose—it's a great sign that drinkers are beginning to appreciate the value of fine tequila.

1½ oz. Sauza Conmemorativo tequila
1 oz. Cointreau
2 oz. fresh lemon juice
salt (for the glass)

Add all the ingredients to a shaker filled with ice. Shake sharply and strain into a salt-rimmed, frosted martini glass.

porfidio single barrel perfecta

Porfidio has long been a much-coveted tequila, predominantly due to the beauty of its designer bottles. The skillfully handblown bottle shows off a glass saguaro cactus standing inside (which does nothing to upturn the myth that tequila is made from cactus!). In fairness, the tequila they make is rather good, too.

2 oz. Porfidio Single Barrel Añejo tequila
1 oz. Cointreau
1 oz. fresh lime juice

Add all the ingredients to a shaker filled with ice. Shake sharply and strain into a frosted margarita glass.

lo mayor de sauza

Sauza are the second biggest tequila producers in the world and the Galardon Gran Reposado gives us a reason to understand why. Delicious!

1½ oz. Sauza Galardon Gran Reposado tequila
1 oz. Cointreau
2 oz. fresh lime juice
lime wedge, to garnish
salt (for the glass)

Add all the ingredients to a shaker filled with ice. Shake sharply and strain into a salt-rimmed rocks glass.

24 carat gold reserva

200th anniversary José Cuervo Gran Reserva de la Familia is one of my favorite sipping tequilas, and it would seem sacrilegious to mix it with anything other than the 150th anniversary cuvée Speciale Centcinqantenaire Grand Marnier.

2 oz. José Cuervo Reserva de la Familia tequila
1½ oz. Centcinqantenaire Grand Marnier
1½ oz. fresh lime juice
salt (for the glass)

Add all the ingredients to a shaker filled with ice. Shake sharply and strain into a frosted margarita glass.

boogie man

This drink's name alludes to a fear that I have heard about many times when it comes to drinking tequila, but we all know the boogie man's not real, right?

1½ oz. Chamucos tequila
1 oz. Cointreau
1½ oz. fresh lime juice
salt (for the glass)

Add all the ingredients to a shaker filled with ice. Shake sharply and strain into a salt-rimmed, frosted margarita glass.

the flavoreds

Bartenders have been adding all sorts of flavors to cocktails for decades, and the margarita is no exception. The margarita is quite a finely balanced cocktail, so don't be too rash with your creativity. Adding fresh fruit to cocktails is always more authentic than using fruit liqueurs, but two things need to be kept in mind when doing so. First, the ripest fruit will yield the most flavorful results; secondly, it is important when using strongly flavored fruits not to overshadow the taste of the tequila.

raspberry torte

A successful cocktail needs to have an effect on all of your cocktail senses. This one looks great on the eye, has a fresh lime and berry fragrance on the nose and, if you can ever bring yourself to consume your work of art, delights the tastebuds.

2 oz. gold tequila
scant oz. Cointreau
scant oz. fresh lime juice
2 oz. raspberry purée

Blend the first three ingredients in a blender along with two scoops of crushed ice for 20 seconds. Pour half the mixture into a margarita glass. Gently layer the raspberry purée over the surface of the drink to create a thin red line. Add the remaining margarita mix over the top and serve with two straws.

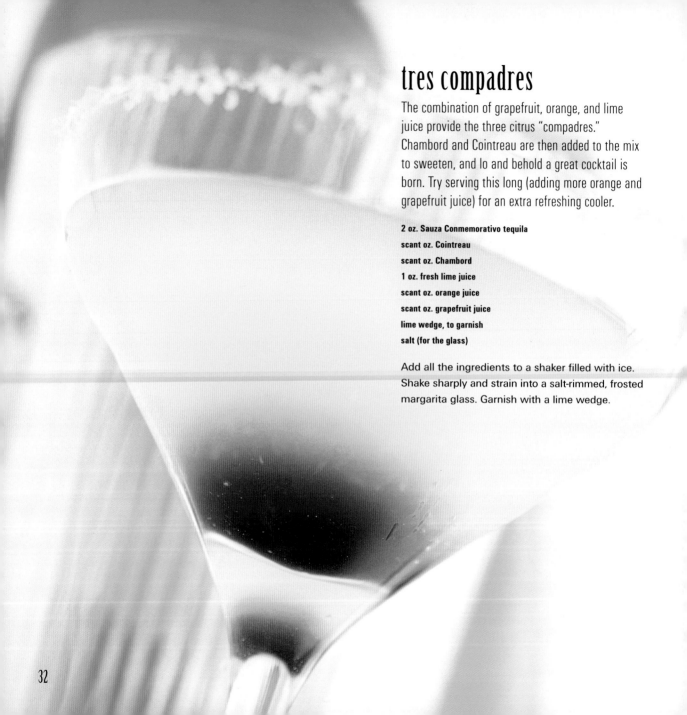

tres compadres

The combination of grapefruit, orange, and lime juice provide the three citrus "compadres." Chambord and Cointreau are then added to the mix to sweeten, and lo and behold a great cocktail is born. Try serving this long (adding more orange and grapefruit juice) for an extra refreshing cooler.

2 oz. Sauza Conmemorativo tequila
scant oz. Cointreau
scant oz. Chambord
1 oz. fresh lime juice
scant oz. orange juice
scant oz. grapefruit juice
lime wedge, to garnish
salt (for the glass)

Add all the ingredients to a shaker filled with ice. Shake sharply and strain into a salt-rimmed, frosted margarita glass. Garnish with a lime wedge.

habañero margarita

This is a drink that I have dabbled with over the years. The first batch I made was served with a glass of milk on the side and an apologetic look on my face. Now I serve it with confidence. Moral of the story: get your mix right before serving and don't leave your chiles infusing for too long!

Habañero infusion
**3 habañero chiles,
  plus 1 to garnish**

bottle of gold tequila

**2 oz. habañero–infused
  gold tequila**

1 oz. Cointreau

1 oz. fresh lime juice

Habañero infusion: Add three fresh habañero chiles to a bottle of gold tequila. Leave for two days or until the chiles lose their color.

Add all the ingredients to a shaker filled with ice. Shake sharply and strain into a frosted margarita glass. Garnish with an habañero chile.

triple gold margarita

Layered with a float of Goldschlager, the Triple Gold Margarita
will bring a touch of splendor to any bar menu. Laced with real
24 carat gold pieces, Goldschlager is a cinnamon-flavored liqueur
that adds considerably to the depth of taste of the cocktail.

2 oz. gold tequila

2 teaspoons Cointreau

2 teaspoons Grand Marnier

scant oz. fresh lime juice

scant oz. Goldschlager

Add all the ingredients except the Goldschlager to a shaker
filled with ice. Shake sharply and strain into a frosted
margarita glass. Float the Goldschlager onto the surface
of the mixture and serve.

red cactus

The fresh raspberries and Chambord in this drink team up to provide a fruity punch that almost masks the flavor of its main liquor. Don't be deceived, there's still plenty of tequila in there!

2 oz. Sauza Gold tequila
scant oz. triple sec
scant oz. Chambord
1½ oz. fresh lime juice
4 fresh raspberries, plus 2 to garnish
lime wedge, to garnish

Add all the ingredients to a blender. Add two scoops of crushed ice and blend for 20 seconds. Pour into a margarita coupette or a hurricane glass. Garnish with a lime wedge and serve with two raspberries.

hibiscus margarita

A deep-purple margarita with the gentle essence of herbed sweetness from the hibiscus. Worth the effort if you aim to impress.

Hibiscus cordial	
2¼ cups sugar	scant oz. hibiscus cordial
4 oz. hibiscus flowers	2 oz. Cuervo Gold tequila
2 quarts of water	scant oz. triple sec
	scant oz. fresh lime juice

Hibiscus cordial: Dissolve the sugar and hibiscus flowers (dried, if out of season) into 2 quarts of water over a low heat. Once the liquid turns a deep red, strain and let cool.

Add all the ingredients to a shaker filled with ice. Shake sharply and strain into a large cocktail glass.

pinarita

The combination of pineapple and tequila results in a truly tropical flavor. I will let you decorate it lavishly despite my open disdain for garish garnishes!

2 oz. gold tequila

scant oz. triple sec

scant oz. fresh lime juice

1 oz. pineapple juice

thin slice of fresh pineapple, to garnish

Add all the ingredients to a blender. Add two scoops of crushed ice and blend for 20 seconds. Pour into a margarita coupette, garnish with a pineapple slice, and serve with two straws.

mangorita

This cocktail is an easy one to make, but very tricky to get right. Mango is a powerful-tasting fruit that can overshadow the taste of tequila entirely. Take care not to add too much mango, especially if it is very ripe. Or do what I do and take care to add a little more tequila!

2 oz. gold tequila
scant oz. triple sec
scant oz. fresh lime juice
1 oz. mango pureé

Add all the ingredients to a shaker filled with ice, shake sharply, and strain into a frosted margarita glass.

blue moon

I'm not a man to hold grudges but I'm not a huge fan
of blue cocktails, they tend to contain blue Curaçao
for its color rather than its taste. In the Blue Moon,
however, blue Curaçao is valid, as the liqueur is
orange-flavored Curaçao, much like triple sec.

2 oz. Sauza Hornitos tequila
1 oz. blue Curaçao
tablespoon fresh lime juice
2 scoops lemon sorbet or sherbet

Add all the ingredients to a blender. Blend for
20 seconds and pour into a margarita glass.

green iguana

The combination of melon and tequila work perfectly here. I have chosen to use Midori in this recipe since fresh melon doesn't have the necessary sweetness to balance the drink.

1¼ oz. Sauza Hornitos tequila
1 oz. Midori
1 oz. fresh lime juice
1 oz. Cointreau
lime wedge, to garnish

Add the all ingredient to a shaker filled with ice. Shake sharply and strain into a rocks glass.

berry margarita

Anything from strawberries to cranberries, blueberries to raspberries can be used in this recipe. Choose your own combination of seasonal berries for subtle variations.

2 oz. gold tequila
scant oz. triple sec
scant oz. fresh lime juice
dash of crème de mure
seasonal berries of your choice, plus extra to garnish

Add all the ingredients to a blender. Add two scoops of crushed ice and blend for 20 seconds. Pour into a margarita coupette and garnish with a berry.

prickly pear margarita

The prickly pear has become *de rigueur* in cocktails and makes a great addition to the margarita. The average pear doesn't always contain enough flavor to carry the drink off so it's well worth spending that bit of extra time looking for the prickly pears.

2 oz. silver tequila
scant oz. triple sec
scant oz. lime juice
dash of grenadine
1 oz. prickly pear purée
thin slice of pear, to garnish

Add all the ingredients to a shaker filled with ice. Shake sharply and strain into a frosted margarita glass. Garnish with a sliver of pear.

the substitutions

Substituting the liquor in a tried and tested recipe is a great way to discover a new drink. Tequila has the ability to lend a great deal to a cocktail—try using an aged tequila for an even more complex spectrum of flavors. When experimenting with this method, ask yourself the following questions: Does the drink mix well with cream? What balance of citrus and sweet tastes best? What other ingredients work well with this liquor?

herba buena

This is a variation on the Cuban classic, the Mojito. Pack the glass with crushed ice and this cocktail makes the perfect summer drink. Add a little extra sugar for the sweeter tooth or a little more lime for that citrus twist.

2 oz. gold tequila
tablespoon fresh lime juice
brown rock sugar cube
5 mint sprigs, plus 1 to garnish
soda water

Muddle all the ingredients, apart from the soda, in a highball glass using a bonzer spoon. Add crushed ice, muddle again, and top up with soda. Stir gently, garnish with a mint sprig, and serve with two straws.

conmemorativo

Championed by New York band the Fun Lovin' Criminals, this is a high-maintenance cocktail, based on the Caipirinha.

1 lime
2 brown rock sugar cubes
2 oz. Sauza Conmemorativo tequila

Cut the lime into 8 wedges, squeeze and drop them into a rocks glass, with the two sugar cubes. Add the tequila and muddle again to dissolve the sugar. Serve with two short straws.

tequila rickey

A long tequila cooler based on one of the oldest documented cocktails, the Collins. Add plenty of lime and sugar to ensure the drink has the balance and depth of taste it deserves.

2 oz. gold tequila
1 oz. fresh lime juice
tablespoon simple syrup
soda water
lime wedge, to garnish

Build all the ingredients in a highball glass filled with ice. Stir gently, garnish with a lime wedge, and serve with two straws.

rude cosmopolitan

The Rude Cosmopolitan earned its name following an evening that began well enough, but descended into heated debate. The tone of the evening changed when the switch was made from drinking vodka to tequila—hence the name.

2 oz. gold tequila
scant oz. Cointreau
scant oz. fresh lime juice
1½ oz. cranberry juice
orange zest, to garnish

Add all the ingredients to a shaker filled with fresh ice. Shake sharply and strain into a frosted martini glass. Garnish with the orange zest.

mezcal margarita

Choosing to substitute mezcal for
tequila will impress any bartender.
Mezcal tends to be more herbaceous
and earthy on the palate—taste
this drink and you'll find yourself
whipped off to Mexico.

2 oz. mezcal

2 teaspoons brandy

2 dashes of Peychaud's Bitters (or Angostura)

scant oz. triple sec

scant oz. fresh lime juice

salt (for the glass)

Add all the ingredients to a shaker
filled with ice. Shake sharply and
strain into a salt-rimmed frosted
margarita glass.

tequilini

Based on the martini, this cocktail is a great way to
serve an aged tequila. Chilled to perfection and softened
by the vermouth—sip and savour your Tequilini.

dash of dry vermouth
2 oz. premium añejo tequila
lime zest, to garnish

Add a dash of vermouth to a mixing glass filled with
ice. Stir gently, then discard any dilution. Add the
tequila and stir again for fifteen seconds. Strain the
mixture into a frosted martini glass and garnish with
a thin zest of lime.

añejo manhattan

The Manhattan and can be made sweet, perfect,
or dry, depending on the ratio of sweet and dry
vermouth. This is the perfect version. Try using
all sweet or all dry vermouth instead.

2 oz. añejo tequila
scant oz. sweet vermouth
scant oz. dry vermouth
dash of Angostura bitters
orange zest, to garnish

Add all the ingredients to a mixing glass filled
with ice. Using a bonzer spoon, stir in a continuous
motion until the mixture is thoroughly chilled.
Strain into a frosted martini glass and garnish
with the orange zest.

tequila colada

This variation slips down the throat as easily as its name rolls off the tongue. Ensure this drink has the right consistency (light and fluffy) by adding crushed ice bit by bit to the blender.

2 oz. gold tequila
scant oz. coconut cream
2 teaspoons heavy cream
⅔ cup pineapple juice
pineapple slice, to garnish

Add all the ingredients to a blender, and add two scoops of crushed ice. Blend for 20 seconds. Pour into a hurricane glass and garnish with a pineapple slice.

lagerita

A fave of mine, this is a drink for the more adventurous among us. It is essential that a dark beer is used. Apologies for the vulgarity of the name but the temptation was too great!!

1 lime
1 oz. Centenario Añejo tequila
brown rock sugar cube
Negra Modello, or other dark beer

Cut the lime into quarters, squeeze and drop them into a highball glass. Add the tequila and the sugar cube and muddle using a bar spoon. Fill the glass with ice and add the dark beer. Muddle again ensuring as much of the sugar has dissolved as possible. Serve with two straws.

bloody maria

If ever I find the need for solace in a hangover cure, the Maria is a worthy adversary to the Mary. Where the vodka in a Mary thins the mixture slightly, the tequila in a Maria binds the ingredients.

2 oz. gold tequila
scant oz. fresh lime juice
cup tomato juice
5 dashes of Tabasco sauce
5 dashes of Worcestershire sauce
pinch of sea salt or kosher
pinch of ground black pepper
pinch of celery salt
lime wedge, to garnish
celery stick, to garnish

Add all the ingredients to a shaker filled with ice. Shake sharply and strain into a highball glass filled with ice. Garnish with a lime wedge and celery.

Tequila has been mixed in traditional Mexican drinks and western variations for years. Some you may love, others you may not thank me for reminding you of. Try the Three Amigos for tequila at its most basic, a Submarine for tequila at its laziest, or a Silk Stocking for tequila at its most decadent. The method of consumption can be as fun as the effect of the drink itself.

other tequila cocktails

los tres amigos

The salt, tequila, and lime method is as ubiquitous as the margarita when it comes to tequila. Recite the immortal words: "lick, sip, suck"—and enjoy!

lime wedge
2 oz. gold tequila
pinch of salt

Hold the lime wedge between the thumb and index finger. Pour the tequila into a shot glass and place the glass in the fleshy part of your hand between the same thumb and finger. Place a pinch of salt onto the top of your hand next to the shot glass. In this order; lick the salt, shoot the tequila, and suck on the lime.

submarine

Forget those age-old constraints of liquor and chaser standing alone. Opt instead for the energy-saving Submarine and let the tequila seep gently from under its upturned shot glass and mingle with the beer before it hits the palate.

2 oz. gold tequila
bottle Mexican beer (Sol)

Pour the tequila into a shot glass. Place the shot glass into an inverted beer glass so that it touches the bottom of the beer glass. Turn the beer glass the right way up so that the shot glass is upside-down but the tequila is still inside. Gently fill the beer glass with the beer, and serve.

silk stocking

This tequila drink was invented during the '20s in
the U.S., at a time when cocktails were often
given names revelling in innuendo and sensuality.

1½ oz. gold tequila

tablespoon white crème de cacao

teaspoon Grenadine

tablespoon heavy cream

2 fresh raspberries, to garnish

Add all the ingredients to a blender. Add two
scoops of crushed ice and blend for 20 seconds.
Pour the mixture into a hurricane glass, garnish
with two raspberries, and serve with two straws.

the sangrita

This drink is the perfect way to savor a fine tequila. Try varying the Sangrita mix, by adding different amounts of orange juice and spices.

2 oz. añejo tequila
Sangrita mix
1 oz. orange juice
1 oz. lime juice
dash of grenadine
dash of Tabasco sauce
dash of Worcestershire sauce

Pour the tequila into a shot glass. Add the remaining ingredients to a separate shot glass, and stir gently. This drink should be tasted tequila first, followed by the Sangrita mix.

salty dog

"Hair of the Salty Dog" is my recommended morning-after fix; it's a simple combination that can cut through the fog of any hangover with its bitter trinity of grapefruit, salt, and tequila. Try adding a dash of hibiscus cordial (see page 37) for a sweetened variation.

2 oz. gold tequila
scant cup grapefruit juice
lime wedge, to garnish
salt (for the rim)

Pour the tequila into a salt-rimmed highball glass filled with ice. Top with grapefruit juice, garnish with a lime wedge, and serve with two straws.

la cucaracha

After creating the perfectly layered shot, La Cucaracha needs to be lit (use a warm glass) and consumed through a straw (from bottom up).

tablespoon kahlua

tablespoon tequila

tablespoon over-proof rum
   (Wray & Nephew)

Layer the liquors one on top of the other using the flat end of a barspoon. Place a straw into the mixture and light the surface liquid. The drink must be drunk before the flame melts the straw.

moppet

Although some may say this wicked combination has had its day, you'll agree it's a great way to start an evening with a fizz and a bang. Place a napkin over the glass and swirl the drink, reciting the traditional chant "un, dos, tres, voom!" before slamming.

2 oz. silver tequila
2 oz. lemon soda (e.g., 7-Up)

Pour both ingredients into a rocks glass. Cover the glass with a paper napkin and slam onto a firm surface. Quickly, while the drink is fizzing, drink the mixture. Alternatively, substitute with gold tequila and champagne.

tequila sunrise

A cocktail synonymous with the '70s, bad hair, lava lamps, and cheesy cocktails. Try modernizing the recipe using Chambord instead of the grenadine for more depth. Alternatively, swallow your pride, slip into your flairs, and enjoy.

2 oz. gold tequila
scant oz. grenadine
a scant cup fresh orange juice
orange slice, to garnish

Build the tequila and the orange juice into a highball glass filled with ice. Gently pour the grenadine down the inside of the glass so the syrup fills the bottom. Garnish with a thin orange slice and serve with two straws.

el chupacabre

Translated as "the vampire", the addition of garlic is perhaps unsurprising. Try using gently crushed garlic cloves and freshly ground chilies for extra zing. It's worth playing around with the strengths of the various ingredients before serving this drink to an unsuspecting public!

2 oz. gold tequila
scant cup tomato juice
tablespoon medium-hot red chili purée
** or: 2 tablespoons salsa or pico de gallo**
scant oz. fresh lime juice
large pinch of garlic powder
large pinch of sea salt or kosher salt
fresh mint sprigs, to garnish

Shake all the ingredients in a shaker filled with ice and strain through a sieve into a highball glass filled with ice. Garnish with a sprig of fresh mint.

index

conversion chart

Measures have been rounded up or down slightly to make measuring easier.

Imperial	Metric
½ oz.	12.5 ml
1 oz. (single)	25 ml
2 oz. (double)	50 ml
3 oz.	75 ml
4 oz.	100 ml
5 oz.	125 ml
6 oz.	150 ml
7 oz.	175 ml
8 oz.	200 ml

acknowledgments

Not sure where I found the time for this latest offering with my new-found position as a globetrotting bartender and, for sure, thanks and praise for help and effort are well deserved. Thanks to Alison, my literary mentor. Notably Catherine for making the shoot by far the most enjoyable to date (and with some of the best results) and Miriam whose untiring, gracious acceptance of missed deadlines is worthy of commemoration. When Helen Trent and Mr Lingwood combine, the effects are always magical, thanks to you both. Thanks, also, to Tom Estes at La Perla.

Mum, again, your commitment to the cause has been second to none—just wish we could wean you off that sweet sherry!